365
unique daily
QUOTES

A YEAR OF UPLIFTING YOUR SPIRIT EVERY DAY!

By Beth Elkassih

365 *unique daily* QUOTES

A Year of Uplifting Your Spirit Every Day!

by

Beth Elkassih

Copyright © 2024 by Beth Elkassih

All rights reserved.

This book or any portion thereof may not be reproduced or used in any manner whatsoever without the express written permission of the publisher except for the use of brief quotations in a book review.

First Edition, 2024
Publisher: Zulzan, LLC
ISBN: 978-1-7368363-5-4
2160 Barranca Parkway #1091
Irvine, CA 92606
Contact: 682-552-8687

Email: **beth@madeyousmileback.com**
www.madeyousmileback.com
www.zulzan.com

Introduction

In the journey of life, we often seek inspiration to overcome challenges, to spark creativity, or simply to start our day on a positive note. "**Unique Daily Quotes: A Year of Uplifting Your Spirit Every Day**" is a treasure trove of wisdom, offering a daily dose of motivation through thoughtfully curated sayings that resonate with the human experience.

Each quote in this collection has been curated exclusively by **Beth Elkassih** and selected for its power to ignite a transformation within, to challenge perspectives, and to encourage action toward a life of fulfillment.

This book is more than just a compilation of words; it is a companion for those moments when you need a nudge in the right direction or a reminder of your inner strength. From the uplifting words of "Unique Daily Quotes" spans a diverse range of voices and ideas. Whether you are looking for the courage to pursue your dreams, the strength to face adversity, or the clarity to see the beauty in every day, you will find a quote here that speaks directly to you.

As you turn the pages of "Unique Daily Quotes," allow the wisdom enclosed to seep into your daily life. Let these quotes challenge you, comfort you, and above all, inspire you to live life to the fullest.

Embrace the opportunity to view the world through a different lens each day and discover how a simple collection of words can indeed change your life.

A Year of Uplifting Your Spirit Every Day!

1

Happy Happy New Year! Instead of Making a Resolution... Make a Commitment Instead!

Beth Elkassih

www.madeyousmileback.com

A Year of Uplifting Your Spirit Every Day!

2

The Best Kind of Laughter is Laughing Until You Cry!

Beth Elkassih

3

Stop Doubting Your 'Greatness' and Start Living the Life You Were Born to Live!

Beth Elkassih

www.madeyousmileback.com

A Year of Uplifting Your Spirit Every Day!

4

Live Your Life to the Best of Your Own 'Happy Heart!'

Beth Elkassih

5

The Only Person Who Can Change Your Life, is the One Looking Back in Your Mirror!!

Beth Elkassih

www.madeyousmileback.com

A Year of Uplifting Your Spirit Every Day!

6

Reclaim Your Happiness and Find Yourself Again!

Beth Elkassih

7

It's Okay to Not be Okay and it's Okay to Reach Out for Help...

Beth Elkassih

www.madeyousmileback.com

A Year of Uplifting Your Spirit Every Day!

8

Discover Your Life's Grand Purpose & Double Your Happiness!

Beth Elkassih

9

Turn Your Tears of Sadness Into Tears of Happiness!

Beth Elkassih

www.madeyousmileback.com

A Year of Uplifting Your Spirit Every Day!

10

Our World Needs a Healing... Humanity Needs a Healing!

Beth Elkassih

11

Experience the Magical Touch of Kindness!

Beth Elkassih

www.madeyousmileback.com

A Year of Uplifting Your Spirit Every Day!

12

We Can Be Whoever We Have the Courage to See. Be Brave. Dream Bigger.

Beth Elkassih

13

Grief Never Ends… But it Changes. It's a Passage, Not a Place to Stay Nor a Lack of Faith… It's The Price Of Love.

Beth Elkassih

A Year of Uplifting Your Spirit Every Day!

14

Family is Much More than DNA...Your 'Family' Can Include Close Friends and Even Caring Online Friends Too!

Beth Elkassih

15

Don't Stress... Remember, Do Your Best and Forget About the Rest!

Beth Elkassih

A Year of Uplifting Your Spirit Every Day!

16

Happiness is Totally in Your Hands... Choose!

Beth Elkassih

17

Find Your Inner Peace by Going Underneath the Exterior Chaos!

Beth Elkassih

www.madeyousmileback.com

A Year of Uplifting Your Spirit Every Day!

18

You Are Worth It! Learn to Love Yourself.

Beth Elkassih

19

Wait! Get Inspired! Get Encouraged! Don't Miss Out Another Second!

Beth Elkassih

www.madeyousmileback.com

A Year of Uplifting Your Spirit Every Day!

20

Don't Let Anyone Take Your Happiness Away! Be as Happy as You Want to Be!

Beth Elkassih

21

The Only Person That Can Stop You From Living The Life You Want, is Yourself!

Beth Elkassih

www.madeyousmileback.com

A Year of Uplifting Your Spirit Every Day!

22

Life Isn't About Getting and Having… It's About Giving and Being…

Beth Elkassih

23

Don't Forget to Take Time Out to Enjoy Each Day!

Beth Elkassih

www.madeyousmileback.com

A Year of Uplifting Your Spirit Every Day!

24

Dream Big! Take Charge of Your Life and Know You Are Going to Accomplish Incredible Things Once You Start Believing in Yourself!

Beth Elkassih

25

Never Regret a Day in Your Life. Good Days Give You Happiness and Bad Days Give You Experience...

Beth Elkassih

www.madeyousmileback.com

A Year of Uplifting Your Spirit Every Day!

26

Happiness Strengths...
Zest, Gratitude, Hope, Curiosity & Love!

Beth Elkassih

27

Don't Stop When You're Tired. Stop When You're Done!

Beth Elkassih

www.madeyousmileback.com

A Year of Uplifting Your Spirit Every Day!

28

It's Nice to be Nice...
Let's Learn to be Kinder to One Another...

Beth Elkassih

29

Gratitude Begins
in Your Heart and Manifests Into Kindness!

Beth Elkassih

www.madeyousmileback.com

A Year of Uplifting Your Spirit Every Day!

30

You Know...
Grateful People are
Happy People!

Beth Elkassih

31

You Can't Describe
the Peace You Get After Helping
Someone.

Beth Elkassih

A Year of Uplifting Your Spirit Every Day!

32

Falling Down is an Accident. Staying Down is a Choice...

Beth Elkassih

33

Once in a While, Right in the Middle of an Ordinary Day, Inexplicable Joy Comes Over You!

Beth Elkassih

www.madeyousmileback.com

A Year of Uplifting Your Spirit Every Day!

34

Your Only
Limit is Your Mind -
Dream Big!

Beth Elkassih

35

You are Worth It!
Learn to
Love Yourself!

Beth Elkassih

www.madeyousmileback.com

A Year of Uplifting Your Spirit Every Day!

36

Life Issues…
Are You Living or Are You Just Existing?!?

Beth Elkassih

37

Miracles Happen…
in the
Most Unexpected Ways!

Beth Elkassih

www.madeyousmileback.com

A Year of Uplifting Your Spirit Every Day!

38

Gratitude + Intentional Kindness Equals Sustained Happiness!

Beth Elkassih

39

On Grieving... There are Some Who Bring a Light So Great That Even After They Have Gone, their Light Remains. Blessings to Them.

Beth Elkassih

www.madeyousmileback.com

A Year of Uplifting Your Spirit Every Day!

40

Remember... All Successful Breakthrus Always Start with a 'Break' From Your Old Ways of Thinking.

Beth Elkassih

41

Relieve Your Emotional Pain by Intentional Prayer.

Beth Elkassih

A Year of Uplifting Your Spirit Every Day!

42

Yes! Intentionally Choose the Happiness of the Moment, Over the Pain of the Past!

Beth Elkassih

43

A Miracle is God Reaching Out to us to Believe!

Beth Elkassih

www.madeyousmileback.com

A Year of Uplifting Your Spirit Every Day!

44

Touch With Your Hearts...
Touch With Your Souls...
Touch with Love.

Beth Elkassih

45

You're Stronger Than You Realize.
You've Survived This Before... This
Feeling Will Pass.

Beth Elkassih

www.madeyousmileback.com

A Year of Uplifting Your Spirit Every Day!

46

Think About It... One Day... One Event... Can Change Everything!

Beth Elkassih

47

Life Always Offers You a Second Chance... it's Called Tomorrow!

Beth Elkassih

www.madeyousmileback.com

A Year of Uplifting Your Spirit Every Day!

48

Sometimes It's Best To Remain Silent and… Smile!

Beth Elkassih

49

There's Nothing Wrong with being 'Silly' Once in Awhile!

Beth Elkassih

www.madeyousmileback.com

A Year of Uplifting Your Spirit Every Day!

50

The Most Powerful Kindness is When Given to Those Who are Unkind.

Beth Elkassih

51

Every Day, Every Hour, Every Second You Spend Time With 1 Person... **You!** You Are Your Best Investment. Be Your Best Friend!

Beth Elkassih

www.madeyousmileback.com

A Year of Uplifting Your Spirit Every Day!

52

Don't Just be a Dreamer... be an Achiever!

Beth Elkassih

53

Good Humor is Tonic for Mind & Body. It is the Best Antidote for Anxiety & Depression. It Lightens the Human Burden...

Beth Elkassih

www.madeyousmileback.com

A Year of Uplifting Your Spirit Every Day!

54

Don't Stop Believing that Something 'Wonderful' is About to Happen!

Beth Elkassih

55

Passion Lights the Fire Towards Ultimate Happiness and Success!

Beth Elkassih

A Year of Uplifting Your Spirit Every Day!

56

'Love' is the Most Powerful
Emotion in the Universe...
Therefore, Let Us Pray!

Beth Elkassih

57

No One is YOU!
That is
your Super Power!

Beth Elkassih

www.madeyousmileback.com

A Year of Uplifting Your Spirit Every Day!

58

Use the Power of 'Love' When Forgiving.

Beth Elkassih

59

Great Blessings Are a Result of Great Perseverance!

Beth Elkassih

www.madeyousmileback.com

A Year of Uplifting Your Spirit Every Day!

60

It Takes Someone Really Special Who Can Make You Smile With Tears in Your Eyes!

Beth Elkassih

61

You're Each Born of Greatness... Never Forget That!

Beth Elkassih

www.madeyousmileback.com

A Year of Uplifting Your Spirit Every Day!

###

I'm Not Going to Tell You It's Going to be Easy... I'm Telling You It's Going to be Worth It!

Beth Elkassih

###

Without Purpose, we Surrender to Living Just a Mediocre and Average Life... Live Purposely!

Beth Elkassih

www.madeyousmileback.com

A Year of Uplifting Your Spirit Every Day!

64

Take the 'Nuggets' of Life Experience From the Past and Turn Them into 'Wisdom' for Living in the Present!

Beth Elkassih

65

YOU Matter. Your Story Matters… Don't be Afraid to Share Your Story!

Beth Elkassih

A Year of Uplifting Your Spirit Every Day!

66

Are You Really Happy or Are You Just Comfortable?

Beth Elkassih

67

When You Experience the Thrill of a 'Come Back,' It is the Most Satisfying of Feelings!

Beth Elkassih

A Year of Uplifting Your Spirit Every Day!

68

When You Get Overwhelmed or
Tired, Learn to Rest...
Not to Quit!

Beth Elkassih

69

Success is the 'Character' you Build
After the 3rd or 4th Try....
or Even the 99th Try... 'Persist'!

Beth Elkassih

A Year of Uplifting Your Spirit Every Day!

70

Sometimes You Need to Close Your Eyes in Order to 'See' and 'Feel' the Real Beauty of the World!

Beth Elkassih

71

Create Your Own Special Type of 'Rainbow' Every Day!

Beth Elkassih

A Year of Uplifting Your Spirit Every Day!

72

Tears are 'God's Heart Shield Wipers'. They Clear the Pain From Our Heart so we can See our Path More Clearly!

Beth Elkassih

73

We're Put on This Earth to Achieve Our Greatest Self, to Live Out our Purpose and do it Courageously!

Beth Elkassih

www.madeyousmileback.com

A Year of Uplifting Your Spirit Every Day!

74

Be the First to Say 'Hello'... Be the First to Offer 'Help'...
Be the First to Offer 'Hope!!'

Beth Elkassih

75

Every New Day You Get a New Life... Forget all Negative Things and Start a 'New Journey!'

Beth Elkassih

A Year of Uplifting Your Spirit Every Day!

76

You Don't Have to Struggle in Silence! Reach Out!

Beth Elkassih

77

The Moment When You Find Out that Your Struggle is Also Someone Else's Struggle, You Realize You're Not Alone.

Beth Elkassih

www.madeyousmileback.com

A Year of Uplifting Your Spirit Every Day!

78

God Created Humanity in All Colors, Shapes & Cultures... God's Love Does Not Discriminate!

Beth Elkassih

79

Thoughts can be Powerful... They Literally can 'Transform Your Life!'

Beth Elkassih

www.madeyousmileback.com

A Year of Uplifting Your Spirit Every Day!

80

Those who are the 'Happiest,' are Those Who Do The Most for Others!

Beth Elkassih

81

Receiving an Act of 'Kindness' Reminds Oneself They Are... Important & Special!

Beth Elkassih

A Year of Uplifting Your Spirit Every Day!

82

You Don't Have to Struggle in Silence… You Can Always 'Reach Out!'

Beth Elkassih

83

Realize Everyone You Meet is Probably Struggling With Some Kind of Life Issue… So Be Kind… Always!

Beth Elkassih

www.madeyousmileback.com

A Year of Uplifting Your Spirit Every Day!

84

The More You Smile...
The More You Smile...

Beth Elkassih

85

In Times of Life Struggles & Difficulties, One Must Learn to be a 'Phoenix' & Rise Up & be Transformed Into the Person You Were Meant to Be!

Beth Elkassih

www.madeyousmileback.com

A Year of Uplifting Your Spirit Every Day!

86

Happiness is a Form of Courage. Happiness is a Choice!

Beth Elkassih

87

Enduring Emotional Pain and Still Showing Up Takes a Strength Most People Will Never Know!

Beth Elkassih

A Year of Uplifting Your Spirit Every Day!

88

Have You Ever Found Yourself Smiling Just to Stop the Tears From Falling? Turn Your Tears of Sadness into Tears of Happiness.

Beth Elkassih

89

Taking Care of Yourself Doesn't Mean 'You First.'
It Means 'You Too!'

Beth Elkassih

www.madeyousmileback.com

A Year of Uplifting Your Spirit Every Day!

90

Be the Person You Were Born to Be!

Beth Elkassih

91

All I Can Do is the Best I Can Do in Any One Given Day... and That is That!

Beth Elkassih

A Year of Uplifting Your Spirit Every Day!

92

When You Choose Hope,
Then Anything
is Possible!

Beth Elkassih

93

You Must Accept What It Is... You Must Let Go What Was... And You Must Have Faith in What Shall Be!

Beth Elkassih

www.madeyousmileback.com

A Year of Uplifting Your Spirit Every Day!

94

Are You Living Life or Just Existing?

Beth Elkassih

95

Sometimes You Just Have to 'Forgive' People Who Clearly Don't Know Any Better!

Beth Elkassih

www.madeyousmileback.com

A Year of Uplifting Your Spirit Every Day!

96

A 'Miracle' Will Inspire You For Sure… But Do You Truly Realize You Are a Miracle Too!

Beth Elkassih

97

Stop Creating 'To Do Lists' and Start Creating a Plan of Action!

Beth Elkassih

A Year of Uplifting Your Spirit Every Day!

98

Ya Know... Just Because We May be Adults... It Doesn't Mean We Can't Play Too!

Beth Elkassih

99

Do Know That At Any Given Moment, You Always Have The Power to 'Pivot' & Change Your Plans!

Beth Elkassih

www.madeyousmileback.com

A Year of Uplifting Your Spirit Every Day!

100

Just Because the 1st Half of Your Day May be Disappointing…
That Doesn't Mean That the Rest of Your Day Can't Be Amazing!

Beth Elkassih

101

Take Time Out to Savor Each & Every One of Life's Unexpected Moments!

Beth Elkassih

www.madeyousmileback.com

A Year of Uplifting Your Spirit Every Day!

102

Stop Your Would've... Could've... Should've Mindset & Start Living With A Plan of Action.

Beth Elkassih

103

You 'Really' Can do Anything!

Beth Elkassih

A Year of Uplifting Your Spirit Every Day!

104

Always Live the Moment!

Beth Elkassih

105

Get 'Inspired'... 'Dream' Big... 'Imagine!'

Beth Elkassih

www.madeyousmileback.com

A Year of Uplifting Your Spirit Every Day!

106

Are You Carrying Around a 'Clear Conscious?' If Not, Then Please Reconcile.

Beth Elkassih

107

Laugh and Recharge Your Batteries!

Beth Elkassih

www.madeyousmileback.com

A Year of Uplifting Your Spirit Every Day!

108

Empathy + Compassion = Emotional Intelligence

Beth Elkassih

109

Focus on the Goodness of People!

Beth Elkassih

www.madeyousmileback.com

A Year of Uplifting Your Spirit Every Day!

110

Let Serendipity Find You!

Beth Elkassih

111

A Gentle Reminder... Angels Are Among Us...

Beth Elkassih

www.madeyousmileback.com

A Year of Uplifting Your Spirit Every Day!

112

Don't Ever Lose Your SPARKLE!

Beth Elkassih

113

Peace Starts With a Smile!

Beth Elkassih

www.madeyousmileback.com

A Year of Uplifting Your Spirit Every Day!

114

Reboot and Change Your Life!

Beth Elkassih

115

Be the 'True Colors' You Are!

Beth Elkassih

A Year of Uplifting Your Spirit Every Day!

116

Be a Part of Something Bigger!

Beth Elkassih

117

The Day to Forgive is Everyday!

Beth Elkassih

www.madeyousmileback.com

A Year of Uplifting Your Spirit Every Day!

118

Humor is Gifts of Blessings.

Beth Elkassih

119

Practice Self-Care and stay 'Mentally Fit!'

Beth Elkassih

A Year of Uplifting Your Spirit Every Day!

120

Have a 'Serendipity' Type of Day!

Beth Elkassih

121

Be Better Than You Were Yesterday!

Beth Elkassih

A Year of Uplifting Your Spirit Every Day!

122

God Didn't Create You Just to Exist...

Beth Elkassih

123

Miracles Happen Every Day!

Beth Elkassih

www.madeyousmileback.com

A Year of Uplifting Your Spirit Every Day!

124

Think Bigger...
Think Smarter...
Think Higher!

Beth Elkassih

125

It's 'Your'
Turn to Break-Thru
'Barriers!'

Beth Elkassih

A Year of Uplifting Your Spirit Every Day!

126

Smile...
Smile More...
Be Happy!

Beth Elkassih

127

Discover Yourself
by Discovering
Nature!

Beth Elkassih

A Year of Uplifting Your Spirit Every Day!

128

Flowers are
Happiness
Blooming!

Beth Elkassih

129

Stop Just 'Existing'...
Start 'Living!'

Beth Elkassih

A Year of Uplifting Your Spirit Every Day!

130

Every Sunrise Starts a New Beginning!

Beth Elkassih

131

Kindness Equals Humble Greatness!

Beth Elkassih

www.madeyousmileback.com

A Year of Uplifting Your Spirit Every Day!

132

You 'Know' You Got This!

Beth Elkassih

133

Don't Forget to Ask... For Everything!

Beth Elkassih

www.madeyousmileback.com

A Year of Uplifting Your Spirit Every Day!

134

You Matter...

Beth Elkassih

135

Listen to Understand... Not to Just Hear!

Beth Elkassih

www.madeyousmileback.com

A Year of Uplifting Your Spirit Every Day!

136

Healing Starts
In Your Mind...

Beth Elkassih

137

Hope Starts
In Your Heart...

Beth Elkassih

A Year of Uplifting Your Spirit Every Day!

138

Be You...
For You!

Beth Elkassih

139

Never Stop
Praying.

Beth Elkassih

A Year of Uplifting Your Spirit Every Day!

140

Care More...
Do More...

Beth Elkassih

141

Happiness is
Always a Choice!

Beth Elkassih

www.madeyousmileback.com

A Year of Uplifting Your Spirit Every Day!

142

Embrace Forgiveness & Relive!

Beth Elkassih

143

Loved Memories Become Treasures!

Beth Elkassih

www.madeyousmileback.com

A Year of Uplifting Your Spirit Every Day!

144

Are You a Difference Maker?

Beth Elkassih

145

The Best You is Simply You!

Beth Elkassih

A Year of Uplifting Your Spirit Every Day!

146

Kindness Can Be Life-Changing!

Beth Elkassih

147

Beauty Does Not Have to be Seen!

Beth Elkassih

www.madeyousmileback.com

A Year of Uplifting Your Spirit Every Day!

148

Look for the 'Good' in Others.

Beth Elkassih

149

It's Okay to Say 'I'm Sorry'...

Beth Elkassih

A Year of Uplifting Your Spirit Every Day!

150

Live!

Beth Elkassih

151

Love!

Beth Elkassih

www.madeyousmileback.com

A Year of Uplifting Your Spirit Every Day!

152

Kindness in Words Creates Empowerment!

Beth Elkassih

153

True Friends Are 'Family!'

Beth Elkassih

A Year of Uplifting Your Spirit Every Day!

154

Resilience is Sustaining.

Beth Elkassih

155

Self-Care is Soul Nourishing.

Beth Elkassih

www.madeyousmileback.com

A Year of Uplifting Your Spirit Every Day!

156

Laugh Until Someone Smiles!

Beth Elkassih

157

Every Victory is a Celebration!

Beth Elkassih

www.madeyousmileback.com

A Year of Uplifting Your Spirit Every Day!

158

Destiny is Based Upon Decisions...

Beth Elkassih

159

Be Your Own Kind of Beautiful!

Beth Elkassih

A Year of Uplifting Your Spirit Every Day!

160

Don't You Even Think of Quitting!

Beth Elkassih

161

Treasure Beautiful Moments!

Beth Elkassih

www.madeyousmileback.com

A Year of Uplifting Your Spirit Every Day!

162

Oh Yes You Can!

Beth Elkassih

163

Never Stop Doing Your 'Best!'

Beth Elkassih

A Year of Uplifting Your Spirit Every Day!

164

A Habit is 21 Consecutive Efforts!

Beth Elkassih

165

Hugs are Love Wrapped Up!

Beth Elkassih

A Year of Uplifting Your Spirit Every Day!

166

Love is
All Around Us!

Beth Elkassih

167

When You Let Negative Things Go, You Then Make Room for Better Things to Come!

Beth Elkassih

www.madeyousmileback.com

A Year of Uplifting Your Spirit Every Day!

168

Be the One to Smile First!

Beth Elkassih

169

What Are You Waiting For?

Beth Elkassih

A Year of Uplifting Your Spirit Every Day!

170

Appreciate the Flow of Nature.

Beth Elkassih

171

Always Look Out For Another!

Beth Elkassih

www.madeyousmileback.com

A Year of Uplifting Your Spirit Every Day!

172

Charity is Kindness Multiplied.

Beth Elkassih

173

Sometimes it's Ok for Others to be Right...

Beth Elkassih

www.madeyousmileback.com

A Year of Uplifting Your Spirit Every Day!

174

Ignite Your 'Passion!'

Beth Elkassih

175

Angels are All Around Us!

Beth Elkassih

A Year of Uplifting Your Spirit Every Day!

176

Experience Unconditional Love!

Beth Elkassih

177

Knowledge is Power!

Beth Elkassih

www.madeyousmileback.com

A Year of Uplifting Your Spirit Every Day!

178

Successful People Ask Anyways!

Beth Elkassih

179

So What's Stopping You?!?

Beth Elkassih

A Year of Uplifting Your Spirit Every Day!

180

Push Through Your Pain to Love Again!

Beth Elkassih

181

Happiness + Joy Equals Pure Love!

Beth Elkassih

www.madeyousmileback.com

A Year of Uplifting Your Spirit Every Day!

182

Be Your Own Type of Miracle!

Beth Elkassih

183

Trust Your Instincts!

Beth Elkassih

www.madeyousmileback.com

A Year of Uplifting Your Spirit Every Day!

184

Are You a 'Doer'?

Beth Elkassih

185

Break Out in a Spontaneous Smile!

Beth Elkassih

A Year of Uplifting Your Spirit Every Day!

186

Reach Even Further Than the Stars!

Beth Elkassih

187

Good Things Will Always Happen!

Beth Elkassih

www.madeyousmileback.com

A Year of Uplifting Your Spirit Every Day!

188

Have You Experienced a Serendipity Surprise?

Beth Elkassih

189

Be 'Worldly!'

Beth Elkassih

A Year of Uplifting Your Spirit Every Day!

190

Love More!

Beth Elkassih

191

There's Nothing Wrong Being Emotional!

Beth Elkassih

A Year of Uplifting Your Spirit Every Day!

192

Positivity Creates Stability.

Beth Elkassih

193

Get Refreshed Instantly! Drink Cold Water!

Beth Elkassih

A Year of Uplifting Your Spirit Every Day!

194

Release All Negativity!

Beth Elkassih

195

Humanity is Colorblind!

Beth Elkassih

www.madeyousmileback.com

A Year of Uplifting Your Spirit Every Day!

196

You Become Your Choices!

Beth Elkassih

197

Encouragement + Inspiration Equals Hope

Beth Elkassih

www.madeyousmileback.com

A Year of Uplifting Your Spirit Every Day!

198

It's Okay to be Different!

Beth Elkassih

199

Lead More... Follow Less!

Beth Elkassih

A Year of Uplifting Your Spirit Every Day!

200

Be Somebody's Blessing!

Beth Elkassih

201

Paint Your Dream & Follow It!

Beth Elkassih

A Year of Uplifting Your Spirit Every Day!

202

Extend Yourself to Be More!

Beth Elkassih

203

Never... Ever... Forget How Special You Are!

Beth Elkassih

A Year of Uplifting Your Spirit Every Day!

204

Never Lose Hope. This Life Is Worth The 'Struggle!'

Beth Elkassih

205

I Know You Can... But Will You?

Beth Elkassih

A Year of Uplifting Your Spirit Every Day!

206

True Friendship Is Not Seen By The Eyes, It's Seen By The Heart.

Beth Elkassih

207

A Journey Consists Of Many Directions.

Beth Elkassih

A Year of Uplifting Your Spirit Every Day!

208

Be Ordinary...
Be Extraordinary!

Beth Elkassih

209

There's Nothing
Wrong In
Thinking Outside The Box!

Beth Elkassih

www.madeyousmileback.com

A Year of Uplifting Your Spirit Every Day!

210

Sometimes You Just Have To 'Close Your Eyes' And Just Do It!

Beth Elkassih

211

Now! Right This Moment, Smile Like You've Never Before!

Beth Elkassih

www.madeyousmileback.com

A Year of Uplifting Your Spirit Every Day!

212

Actions Speak Louder Than Words!
...
Just Saying!

Beth Elkassih

213

Pursue A
Life
Worth Living!

Beth Elkassih

www.madeyousmileback.com

A Year of Uplifting Your Spirit Every Day!

214

Allow Nature
To Speak...
Then Listen!

Beth Elkassih

215

Live Every
Day With
A Grateful Heart!

Beth Elkassih

www.madeyousmileback.com

A Year of Uplifting Your Spirit Every Day!

216

Real Success Isn't Reached
Without Experiencing Failure First!
...Think About It!

Beth Elkassih

217

Never Doubt Yourself.
Once You Doubt Yourself You Fail...
Believe!

Beth Elkassih

www.madeyousmileback.com

A Year of Uplifting Your Spirit Every Day!

218

Change Your Attitude And Start Looking At The Brighter Side Of Life! Even If It Hurts... Your Eyes!

Beth Elkassih

219

Have You Heard About The 90/10 Rule? 10% Do What 90% Are Not Willing To Do... Are You In The 10% Group?

Beth Elkassih

A Year of Uplifting Your Spirit Every Day!

220

Always Celebrate
The Wins Of Others. Success Is For Everyone!

Beth Elkassih

221

The Formula For Success Is Really Straight Forward. Define Your Goal... Find Who Has Achieved It... Then Do Everything They Did!

Beth Elkassih

A Year of Uplifting Your Spirit Every Day!

222

Sometimes You Just Have To Accept It Is What It Is!

Beth Elkassih

223

It's Okay To Go Back To Square One And Start Again!

Beth Elkassih

www.madeyousmileback.com

A Year of Uplifting Your Spirit Every Day!

224

Remember There's No Competition When 'You' Are Being 'You!'

Beth Elkassih

225

Make Life More Beautiful... Smile!

Beth Elkassih

www.madeyousmileback.com

A Year of Uplifting Your Spirit Every Day!

226

If You Won't Do It, Who Will?

Beth Elkassih

227

So... What Are You Waiting For? Start!

Beth Elkassih

www.madeyousmileback.com

A Year of Uplifting Your Spirit Every Day!

228

Peace Begins With 'Love!'

Beth Elkassih

229

Stop Delaying And Start Doing!

Beth Elkassih

A Year of Uplifting Your Spirit Every Day!

230

Sometimes...
Change
Is Growth!

Beth Elkassih

231

Depression Is Not A Sign Of Weakness. Perhaps It Means You Have Been 'Strong' Far Too Long!

Beth Elkassih

www.madeyousmileback.com

A Year of Uplifting Your Spirit Every Day!

232

Life Is Too Short...
Regret
Nothing!

Beth Elkassih

233

Embrace
The Power Of
Your Faith!

Beth Elkassih

A Year of Uplifting Your Spirit Every Day!

234

Sometimes The Best Advice Will Come From A Stranger... Be Open To Receive!

Beth Elkassih

235

Remember, Just Because You Forgive Someone Doesn't Mean You Have To Forget.

Beth Elkassih

A Year of Uplifting Your Spirit Every Day!

236

Stop Being A 'Worrier' And Start Being A 'Warrior!'

Beth Elkassih

237

Reach Into Your 'Soul' And Find Your Unique 'Greatness!'

Beth Elkassih

A Year of Uplifting Your Spirit Every Day!

238

Sometimes In A Conversation, It's Best To Keep Quiet And Just 'Smile!'

Beth Elkassih

239

If We Don't Tell People How We Feel, How Will They Know?

Beth Elkassih

www.madeyousmileback.com

A Year of Uplifting Your Spirit Every Day!

240

When Your Heart And Soul Are Aligned... The Most Highest Of 'Love' Is Achieved.

Beth Elkassih

241

Appreciate All The
'Goodness'
In Your Life!

Beth Elkassih

A Year of Uplifting Your Spirit Every Day!

242

Embrace Forgiveness And Relive!

Beth Elkassih

243

Let 'Serendipity' Find You!

Beth Elkassih

A Year of Uplifting Your Spirit Every Day!

244

Take A Moment, Pause... And Really Feel The 'Love' Of Your Heart!

Beth Elkassih

245

Think About It. Love Heals 'Everything!'

Beth Elkassih

A Year of Uplifting Your Spirit Every Day!

246

Overcoming Challenges Makes Life Meaningful!

Beth Elkassih

247

What Sets Your 'Soul' On Fire?

Beth Elkassih

www.madeyousmileback.com

A Year of Uplifting Your Spirit Every Day!

248

True Friends Multiply 'Goodness' And Divide Life 'Sorrows!'

Beth Elkassih

249

Authentic Friendship Is Truly 'Inexplicable!'

Beth Elkassih

A Year of Uplifting Your Spirit Every Day!

250

Why Not Rediscover Yourself!?!

Beth Elkassih

251

You Don't Know What You Don't Know! Keep Learning!

Beth Elkassih

www.madeyousmileback.com

A Year of Uplifting Your Spirit Every Day!

252

Explore The Positive Creativity Of Your Mind!

Beth Elkassih

253

The Truth Is The Truth And Will 'Always' Be The Truth!

Beth Elkassih

A Year of Uplifting Your Spirit Every Day!

254

What Do You 'Love' And What Are You Doing About It?

Beth Elkassih

255

Make Each Day The 'Best Day Ever!'

Beth Elkassih

A Year of Uplifting Your Spirit Every Day!

256

Experience The 'Fun' Again... Play Like You're 10 Years Old!

Beth Elkassih

257

Have You Ever Noticed That The Most Talented, Life-Changing And Thought-Provoking People Are One Of A Kind!

Beth Elkassih

A Year of Uplifting Your Spirit Every Day!

258

Only Those Who Have An Open Mind Receives Opportunities, The Closed Minded Doesn't Even Know Have Passed Them By!

Beth Elkassih

259

Focus Your
Energy &
Live 'Large!'

Beth Elkassih

www.madeyousmileback.com

A Year of Uplifting Your Spirit Every Day!

260

Definition Of A Warrior : One With The Willpower To Overcome Any Struggle. Are You A Warrior?

Beth Elkassih

261

There's Nothing Like Experiencing The Powerful Emotion Of 'Tears Of Happiness.'

Beth Elkassih

www.madeyousmileback.com

A Year of Uplifting Your Spirit Every Day!

262

The Best Gesture Of 'Kindness' Is When You Give A Heartfelt Compliment To Someone!

Beth Elkassih

263

If You're Not Obsessed With Your Life, Then You Need To 'Change It!'

Beth Elkassih

www.madeyousmileback.com

A Year of Uplifting Your Spirit Every Day!

264

Everything Happens For A Reason... But Wouldn't It Be Nice To Know The Reason?!?

Beth Elkassih

265

We May Not Always Be At The 'Top Of Our Game', But You Still Must Do The 'Best You Can Do'!

Beth Elkassih

www.madeyousmileback.com

A Year of Uplifting Your Spirit Every Day!

266

Be Persistent... Be Relentless... Be Consistent... And You Will Reach Your Dreams!

Beth Elkassih

267

Without Laughter...
Your Day
Is Not Complete!

Beth Elkassih

A Year of Uplifting Your Spirit Every Day!

268

You're The Average Of The '5 People' You Hang Out With... What Does This Say About You?

Beth Elkassih

269

The Best Feeling Of Happiness Is When You 'Yourself' Make Somebody Else Happy!

Beth Elkassih

www.madeyousmileback.com

A Year of Uplifting Your Spirit Every Day!

270

Never Allow The Thought Of Giving Up To Take Root In Your Mind.

Beth Elkassih

271

Do Know...
Prayer Is The Most Powerful Of All Human Action!

Beth Elkassih

A Year of Uplifting Your Spirit Every Day!

272

The Joy Of Gratitude Is True Happiness!

Beth Elkassih

273

Declutter The Chaos From Your Life!

Beth Elkassih

A Year of Uplifting Your Spirit Every Day!

274

Refind Yourself And Reclaim The Happiness That Is Rightfully Yours!

Beth Elkassih

275

Surround Yourself With Flowers And You Will Smile!

Beth Elkassih

www.madeyousmileback.com

A Year of Uplifting Your Spirit Every Day!

276

Never Underestimate The Power Of Miracles!

Beth Elkassih

277

Those Who Do The Most For Others Are The Ones Who Are The Most Deserving!

Beth Elkassih

www.madeyousmileback.com

A Year of Uplifting Your Spirit Every Day!

278

Exercise Your Mind... It's Just As Important As Your Physical Fitness.

Beth Elkassih

279

Race Should Be Eliminated From The Dictionary And Replaced By Simply 'Humanity.'

Beth Elkassih

A Year of Uplifting Your Spirit Every Day!

280

Are You Doing Your Part In Bringing Kindness Into The World?

Beth Elkassih

281

Sometimes I Find Myself Over-Thinking... But I Also Find Myself Over-Loving.

Beth Elkassih

www.madeyousmileback.com

A Year of Uplifting Your Spirit Every Day!

282

Stop Ever Apologizing For Being Your Authentic Self!

Beth Elkassih

283

Effort Is Attractive!

Beth Elkassih

A Year of Uplifting Your Spirit Every Day!

284

Love Is Simple...
Love
Never Fails!

Beth Elkassih

285

It's Not Gossip
If It's The Truth!

Beth Elkassih

www.madeyousmileback.com

A Year of Uplifting Your Spirit Every Day!

286

Are You Living With Passion?

Beth Elkassih

287

Sometimes Saying 'No' Means Saying 'Yes' For Yourself!

Beth Elkassih

www.madeyousmileback.com

A Year of Uplifting Your Spirit Every Day!

288

Self-Care Must Take Place First In Order To 'Care' For Others!

Beth Elkassih

289

Crossing The Finish Line To Your Goals Is Not A 'Race!'

Beth Elkassih

www.madeyousmileback.com

A Year of Uplifting Your Spirit Every Day!

290

Believe It
And You
Can Achieve It!

Beth Elkassih

291

With Prayer,
Anything
Is Possible!

Beth Elkassih

A Year of Uplifting Your Spirit Every Day!

292

Charity Begins At Home.

Beth Elkassih

293

Give More... Live More!

Beth Elkassih

A Year of Uplifting Your Spirit Every Day!

294

When You Give Charity... Your Blessings Are Multiplied.

Beth Elkassih

295

Charity Starts In Your Heart.

Beth Elkassih

A Year of Uplifting Your Spirit Every Day!

296

At The End Of The Day, How You Treat People Ultimately Tells All. Integrity Is Everything!

Beth Elkassih

297

Be Open To An Extraordinary Life!

Beth Elkassih

A Year of Uplifting Your Spirit Every Day!

298

Sometimes Unexpected Events End Up Being Life Blessings.

Beth Elkassih

299

Safeguard Your Joy! Don't Let Anyone Take It Away From You!

Beth Elkassih

www.madeyousmileback.com

A Year of Uplifting Your Spirit Every Day!

300

Experience The Serendipity Joy Of Appreciating Nature.

Beth Elkassih

301

Hope ... The Game-Changing Emotion! Expect Something Wonderful!

Beth Elkassih

www.madeyousmileback.com

A Year of Uplifting Your Spirit Every Day!

302

Faith Should Be The Highest Of Priorities!

Beth Elkassih

303

Never Give Up... Never Surrender... Persevere!

Beth Elkassih

A Year of Uplifting Your Spirit Every Day!

304

Life Is Too Short!
Regret Nothing!

Beth Elkassih

305

Never Doubt Yourself!
Once You Doubt,
You Fail!

Beth Elkassih

A Year of Uplifting Your Spirit Every Day!

306

Make Your Life The Way You Want It To Be!

Beth Elkassih

307

To Get Anything Done In The World, You Must First Love Yourself!

Beth Elkassih

www.madeyousmileback.com

A Year of Uplifting Your Spirit Every Day!

308

A Good Salesman Knows That A 'No' Is One Step Closer To 'Yes!'

Beth Elkassih

309

Be Original! Be Extraordinary! Stand Out From The Rest!

Beth Elkassih

A Year of Uplifting Your Spirit Every Day!

310

It's Okay To Go Back To Square One And Try Again!

Beth Elkassih

311

Change Your Mood! Stand Up, Look Up, and Simply Smile & Be Grateful For Life!

Beth Elkassih

A Year of Uplifting Your Spirit Every Day!

312

In The Great Scheme of Things, When Disappointed, Does It Really Matter? Keep Moving Forward.

Beth Elkassih

313

Don't Ever Apologize For Doing The Right Thing!

Beth Elkassih

A Year of Uplifting Your Spirit Every Day!

314

Always Be Humble In Everything You Do!

Beth Elkassih

315

Strive To Be Better Each Day!

Beth Elkassih

A Year of Uplifting Your Spirit Every Day!

316

Sometimes You Just Have To Accept 'It Is What It Is!'

Beth Elkassih

317

There's Nothing Wrong In Thinking 'Outside The Box!'

Beth Elkassih

www.madeyousmileback.com

A Year of Uplifting Your Spirit Every Day!

318

Never Settle For Being Mediocre! Always Strive For The Highest Level!

Beth Elkassih

319

Never... Ever... Settle When You Know You Can Have Better!

Beth Elkassih

A Year of Uplifting Your Spirit Every Day!

320

Sometimes The Best Advice Will Come From A Stranger... Be Open To Receive.

Beth Elkassih

321

One Will Never Get Ahead In This Life Unless They Learn The Power Of Prayer.

Beth Elkassih

A Year of Uplifting Your Spirit Every Day!

322

Don't Overthink Something... Instead Reflect.

Beth Elkassih

323

When You Think About It, Giving And Receiving Love Is Really What We're All On This Planet For...

Beth Elkassih

A Year of Uplifting Your Spirit Every Day!

324

Don't Forget - Your Legacy Shall Be Your Forever Imprint.

Beth Elkassih

325

Do You Prosper In Happiness?

Beth Elkassih

A Year of Uplifting Your Spirit Every Day!

326

When You Align Your Soul To Your Faith, Extraordinary Things Happen!

Beth Elkassih

327

When You're At A Loss On What To Do In A Difficult Situation, Give To Charity.

Beth Elkassih

www.madeyousmileback.com

A Year of Uplifting Your Spirit Every Day!

328

Resilience Is The Script That Turns Our Struggles Into Triumph!

Beth Elkassih

329

Loyalty Is The Silent Promise That Echoes Through Our Actions.

Beth Elkassih

www.madeyousmileback.com

A Year of Uplifting Your Spirit Every Day!

330

Actions Speak Louder Than Words... What Does 'Your' Actions Say About You?

Beth Elkassih

331

The Truth Is The Truth And Will Always Be The Truth!

Beth Elkassih

www.madeyousmileback.com

A Year of Uplifting Your Spirit Every Day!

332

To Become A Leader, You First Need To Learn To Be A Team Player!

Beth Elkassih

333

Honor Is Everything!

Beth Elkassih

A Year of Uplifting Your Spirit Every Day!

334

The Art Of Listening
Is More
Valuable Than Speaking.

Beth Elkassih

335

Appreciate All
The Goodness
In Your Life!

Beth Elkassih

www.madeyousmileback.com

A Year of Uplifting Your Spirit Every Day!

336

Embrace The Power Of Your Faith!

Beth Elkassih

337

Find The Beauty In The Ordinary!

Beth Elkassih

A Year of Uplifting Your Spirit Every Day!

338

Stop Doubting Yourself & Start Believing You Can!

Beth Elkassih

339

A Friendly Reminder... You're Amazing... You're Awesome... You're Worth It!

Beth Elkassih

A Year of Uplifting Your Spirit Every Day!

340

When You Have 'Inner Peace,' You Then Will Be In Harmony With Your Soul.

Beth Elkassih

341

Don't Overthink Things...
Lead With
Your 'Heart!'

Beth Elkassih

A Year of Uplifting Your Spirit Every Day!

342

When You Give Someone A Chance To Help You, You're Also Giving Them An Opportunity To Feel Valued!

Beth Elkassih

343

There's Nothing Wrong In Walking Away From 'Toxic' Family Members... You Can Love Them From A Distance!

Beth Elkassih

www.madeyousmileback.com

A Year of Uplifting Your Spirit Every Day!

344

Don't Take Life For Granted... Sleepwalking Until Something Awakens You... Live Life To The Fullest!

Beth Elkassih

345

Whomever Has A 'Why' To Live For; Can Bear Any 'How'... Just Saying!

Beth Elkassih

A Year of Uplifting Your Spirit Every Day!

346

Give Yourself Hope A 2nd Chance... & You Will Learn How To 'Fly' Again!

Beth Elkassih

347

If I Could Give You One Gift... It Would Be To Give You The Ability To See How 'Special' You Are!

Beth Elkassih

A Year of Uplifting Your Spirit Every Day!

348

Sometimes You Just Need To Get Out Of Your Own Way!

Beth Elkassih

349

Sometimes The Struggles We Go Thru In Life Puts Us Directly On A Path Towards A Better Life!

Beth Elkassih

www.madeyousmileback.com

A Year of Uplifting Your Spirit Every Day!

350

Find Gratitude & Joy, Then 'Happiness' Will Be Yours!

Beth Elkassih

351

Kindness Is One Of The Most Powerful Emotions Of 'Love'... Share Kindness As Much As You Can!

Beth Elkassih

A Year of Uplifting Your Spirit Every Day!

352

Be A 'Beacon' In Someone's Darkness!

Beth Elkassih

353

Never Ever Let Anyone Tell You That Your Dreams Are 'Too Big!'

Beth Elkassih

www.madeyousmileback.com

A Year of Uplifting Your Spirit Every Day!

354

You Alone Have The Power To Take Your Life In New Directions!

Beth Elkassih

355

Greatness & Goodness Was Created In Everyone! Step Into The Gifts God Gave You!

Beth Elkassih

A Year of Uplifting Your Spirit Every Day!

356

Do Know That Charity & Prayers Multiplies The Blessings From God!

Beth Elkassih

357

Stress We Experience Isn't Caused By Having Too Much To Do… It Comes From Not Finishing What We Started!

Beth Elkassih

www.madeyousmileback.com

A Year of Uplifting Your Spirit Every Day!

358

If You Think Positive... If You Are Positive... Then You Will Be Positive!

Beth Elkassih

359

Believe In The Power Of Imagination... To Release The Truth Within Us!

Beth Elkassih

A Year of Uplifting Your Spirit Every Day!

360

The First Secret Of Finding Happiness Is Loving Yourself!

Beth Elkassih

361

Be Courageous To 'Power Thru' Your Pain When Going Thru Life Struggles!

Beth Elkassih

www.madeyousmileback.com

A Year of Uplifting Your Spirit Every Day!

362

Disappointments Are Just God's Way Of Saying He Has Something 'Better' Waiting For You!

Beth Elkassih

363

Be Patient...
Live Life...
Have Faith!

Beth Elkassih

A Year of Uplifting Your Spirit Every Day!

364

One Of The Most Powerful Acts Of Kindness Is Seeing The Best In Others When They Can't See It In Themselves!

Beth Elkassih

365

When You Have Sincere Gratitude In Your Life... You Have Abundant Happiness!

Beth Elkassih

www.madeyousmileback.com

A Year of Uplifting Your Spirit Every Day!

Bonus Quote for Leap Years!

366

Those Born In A Leap Year, Graced With A Rare Rhythm Of Time - Every Four Years, A True Moment To Shine.

Beth Elkassih

www.madeyousmileback.com

ABOUT THE AUTHOR

Beth Elkassih is a prolific professional blogger and creator of the blog entitled: **"Made You Smile Back"** (https://madeyousmileback.com) which was created in October 2018. Beth is a curated contributor for Medium and for Babyboomer.org and has written over 350+ blog articles on the subjects of 'happiness' and promoting mental health advocacy in her writings.

In 2019, she wrote her 1st best-selling book on Amazon, "**The Power of Unexpected Miracles**". This book is about the true story of the survival of her 3rd daughter and herself during birth at age 41 and the series of 'blessings in disguise' or 'miracles' that occurred during her recovery from acute post-partum depression.

'**The Power of Unexpected Miracles**' ended up being a Best Seller on Amazon in two categories and an International Best Seller in Australia, the United Kingdom, and Canada in 2019.

Her 2nd best-seller, "**I Just Want To Be Happy Again**" was published in 2021, also on Amazon. This is a collection of 14 of her most popular blog articles up to 2021. A 2nd edition shall be forthcoming in 2024.

In addition, she is the co-author (with Umair Qureshi) of three journals - '**The Ultimate Happiness Journal**', The Ultimate Journal of Gratitude' and 'Sacred Love' -- all available on Amazon.

Beth Elkassih is the proud creator of the growing Facebook Group, Achieving Happiness https://facebook.com/groups/achievinghappiness/ This private group was created as a 'no judgment zone' for those needing daily encouragement to achieve their own personal happiness levels.

Beth Elkassih is very proud to be a certified 'facilitator' for NAMI (National Alliance of Mental Illness) in Tarrant County, Texas. She is available for Happiness Life Coaching and as a Motivational Speaker.

Since 2006, Beth is also a licensed Realtor for the Dallas/Fort Worth Texas Metroplex and is currently married and lives in the Dallas/Fort Worth Texas area.

THANK YOU FOR READING MY BOOK!

Thank you for allowing me to share with you these 365 unique and original daily quotes to inspire you and help change your life.

If you enjoyed reading these quotes and you find several resonate with you, I welcome you to visit my blog site, **"Made You Smile Back"** (www.madeyousmileback.com) to read more.

Reviews are most welcome and also very much appreciated. They can be left on Amazon and/or Good Reads or you can feel free to email me at **beth@madeyousmileback.com**

Plans are in the works to create a 2nd Edition as a 'spiraled' desktop calendar version in 2024 as well.

Be sure to subscribe to my blog so you can be one of the first to know about the upcoming launch date. For doing so, you can receive a free e-book, '**Reclaim Your Happiness Workbook**'. For convenience, below is the QR code to scan and sign up to receive instantly:

As an avid mental health awareness advocate, I try to do my part in 'removing the stigma of mental illness' through my writings. Please follow me on all social media:

https://facebook.com/madeyousmileback
https://instagram.com/madeyousmileback
https://tiktok.com/@madeyousmileback
https://pinterest.com/madeyousmileback
https://linkedin.com/in/beth-elkassih-made-you-smile-back

Many Blessings!
Beth Elkassih
Email: **beth@madeyousmileback.com**

A Year of Uplifting Your Spirit Every Day!

A Year of Uplifting Your Spirit Every Day!

www.madeyousmileback.com

A Year of Uplifting Your Spirit Every Day!

www.madeyousmileback.com

A Year of Uplifting Your Spirit Every Day!

www.ingramcontent.com/pod-product-compliance
Lightning Source LLC
Chambersburg PA
CBHW071438080526
44587CB00014B/1898